4th Grade

Samantha Smith

A JOURNEY FOR PEACE

BY ANNE GALICICH

DILLON PRESS, INC.
Minneapolis, Minnesota 55415

Photographic Acknowledgments

The photographs are reproduced through the courtesy of Whitney Draper (pages 30, 54, 55, 63, 66); *Portland Press Herald*, Gordon Chibroski (page 58); TASS/SOVFOTO (pages 6, 34, 37, 39, 42, 45, 46, 60, 67, cover); United Nations (page 27); and UPI/Bettman Archives (pages 16, 23, 48).

Library of Congress Cataloging in Publication Data

Galicich, Anne.
Samantha Smith : a journey for peace.

(Taking part)
Includes index.
SUMMARY: Describes Samantha Smith's historic trip to the Soviet Union at the invitation of the Soviet leader, Yuri Andropov, and her subsequent travels and speeches promoting peace and understanding among nations.
1. Smith Samantha. Journey to the Soviet Union—Juvenile literature.   2. Soviet Union—Description and travel—1970-—Juvenile liteature.   3. Peace—Juvenile literature.   4. Smith, Samantha—Juvenile literature. [1. Smith, Samantha. 2. Peace.   3. Soviet Union—Description and travel.]   I. Title.
DK29.G34   1987   914.7'04853   87-13614
ISBN 0-87518-367-0

Dillon Press, Inc., 242 Portland Avenue South
Minneapolis, Minnesota 55415

Printed in the United States of America

3 4 5 6 7 8 9 10 96 95 94 93 92 91 90 89

CONTENTS

SAMANTHA SMITH

In 1983, eleven-year-old Samantha Smith made history when she traveled to the Soviet Union at the invitation of Yuri Andropov, the Soviet leader. Samantha's journey for peace took her to Moscow, Artek—a children's summer camp on the Black Sea—and Leningrad. She found that Soviet young people were much like Americans in their desire for peace.

After her trip Samantha continued to travel and speak out for international understanding among nations. From her native state of Maine to Japan, she made appearances on television and spoke to large gatherings of people about the need for peace among individuals and nations. In 1985, just as Samantha was beginning a career as an actress, she and her father were killed in a plane crash on their way back home to Maine. Samantha's mother, Jane Smith, established the Samantha Smith Foundation to carry on the work her daughter had so bravely begun.

1 My name is Samantha Smith

If you opened a newspaper from the spring or summer of 1983, you might see a photograph of a friendly looking girl with straight brown hair down to her shoulders, a sprinkle of freckles across her nose, and a big smile. If you read the caption underneath the photograph, or the article that went with it, you would discover some other facts about her. Probably the first thing you would learn would be her name—Samantha Smith. You would find out that in 1983 she was ten years old, she was in the fifth grade, and she lived in a small town with her parents, Arthur and Jane, and her dog Kim. You might also learn that she liked field hockey, softball, roller-skating, and reading, or that she enjoyed science but had trouble with math. All in all, you might think that Samantha sounded a lot like your friends. Then why would you find an article about Samantha in a 1983 newspaper?

Like most children, Samantha watched her share of television. It seemed to her that on almost every channel there was something about nuclear bombs. She learned that nuclear weapons, which have been developed by both the United States and the Soviet Union, are many times more powerful than regular weapons. Once she tuned into a public television program and listened to scientists explain how a war fought with nuclear weapons would destroy both the earth and its atmosphere.

Finally, in November of 1982, Samantha sat down and wrote a letter to Yuri Andropov, the new Soviet leader. She told him she was worried about the possibility of a nuclear war between the United

States and the Soviet Union. And that, wrote Samantha in her book, *Journey to the Soviet Union*, is how "the whole thing started."

Samantha Reed Smith lived in Maine all her life. Maine is a rather large state, mostly covered by pine forests, at the top of New England. If you looked at a map of the United States, you would notice that Maine borders only one other state— New Hampshire. Its two other neighbors are Canada and the Atlantic Ocean, where its steep, rocky shore meets the sea.

Many of the places in Maine have Indian names. In fact, the county where Samantha was born, Aroostook, has such a name. Aroostook County forms the part of Maine that juts up into Canada. Samantha was born on June 29, 1972, in Houlton, a town not too far from the Canadian border. Arthur, her father, was born in New York

City and grew up in West Virginia, where he met Jane, Samantha's mother. When Arthur got a job as an instructor at Ricker College in Houlton, the Smiths moved from West Virginia all the way up to the northernmost tip of Maine.

Samantha went to kindergarten in Hodgdon, a nearby town. She was an active little girl who especially enjoyed gymnastics. When she was five years old, Samantha wrote her first letter to the head of a nation, Queen Elizabeth of England. In the letter, Samantha simply expressed her admiration for the queen. In reply, Samantha received a thank-you note from the queen's lady-in-waiting, who wrote that she had been "ordered" by the queen to answer Samantha's letter. Though it wasn't the most personal response, Samantha was happy to receive any answer from such a famous person.

In 1980, when Samantha had finished the second grade, the Smiths moved south to Manchester, Maine. Manchester is located at the state's center, just outside the city of Augusta, Maine's capital. Arthur Smith taught literature and writing to students at the University of Maine at Augusta. Jane Smith worked in Augusta as a social worker with the Maine Department of Human Services. Her job was to help poor children and their families. While her parents worked, Samantha attended Manchester Elementary School, which was just a short bus ride from her home.

In November 1982, not long after she started fifth grade, Samantha wrote her letter to Yuri Andropov. What made her write the letter? One day, she and her mother sat down together to read an article about relations between the United States and the Soviet Union. Jane Smith thought that reading the story would help answer some of Samantha's questions about the bad feelings between the two countries. But after they had read the story, Samantha was still confused. Neither the American nor the Soviet people, it seemed to her, wanted war. So who would start a war, and why? Samantha suggested that her mother write to the new Soviet leader, Andropov, to find out. Jane Smith replied, "Why don't *you?*"

Samantha thought about it and decided that a letter would be a good idea. The man on the magazine cover, with his white hair and glasses, looked a little stern. Still, as Samantha said later, "I thought I'd get to know him better if I wrote to him and he wrote back."

Samantha's letter to the Soviet leader was only a paragraph long. Although she owned a typewriter, Samantha chose to write the letter out by hand to make it more personal. This is what it said:

Dear Mr. Andropov,

My name is Samantha Smith. I am ten years old. Congratulations on your new job. I have been worrying about Russia and the United States getting into a nuclear war. Are you going to vote to have a war or not? If you aren't please tell me how you are going to help to not have a war. This question you do not have to answer, but I would like to know why you want to conquer the world or at least our country. God made the world for us to live together in peace and not to fight.

Sincerely,

Samantha Smith

Samantha put the letter in the envelope and addressed the envelope to Mr. Yuri Andropov/ The Kremlin/Moscow/U.S.S.R. The address that Samantha used needs a bit of explanation. Imagine that a Soviet child wrote a letter to the president of the United States in 1982, the same year that Samantha wrote her letter to Yuri Andropov.

The envelope that the Soviet child addressed might look like this: Mr. Ronald Reagan/The White House/Washington, D.C./U.S.A.

While the long Maine winter of 1982 was passing, Samantha nearly forgot about the letter she had sent to Andropov. Then, in April 1983, she was suddenly called into the principal's office at Manchester Elementary. She couldn't think of anything at all she had done wrong. As it turned out, a phone call, and not an angry principal, was waiting for her. On the other end of the line was a reporter from United Press International. UPI, as it is known, is an agency that distributes news stories and photographs to newspapers and radio and television stations all over the world.

The reporter from UPI wanted to know whether Samantha had in fact written a letter to Yuri Andropov. He told her that he had seen a copy of her letter in *Pravda*, a Soviet newspaper. Imagine how puzzled and surprised Samantha must have been when she heard her letter had been published—and before she knew whether Andropov had received it!

When she got home that day, she wrote another letter, this time to the Soviet ambassador in Washington. Since the ambassador represented the Soviet government in the United States, Samantha thought he might be able to explain things to her. A few days later she received a telephone call from a man at the Soviet embassy. He said that a letter from Andropov, written in English, was on its way to her. On April 25, on her way to school, Samantha stopped by the Manchester post office with her father to pick up the letter from Yuri Andropov.

Samantha Smith shows the letter from Soviet leader Yuri Andropov to reporters at her home.

2 Letter-writing works

April 25, 1983, was a Monday, and the trip to the post office had already put Samantha behind schedule. She had just enough time to skim the letter from the Soviet leader before stepping out of her father's car at Manchester Elementary School.

That afternoon, when school was over, she took her usual seat on the school bus, and the driver took his usual route to her house. But instead of stepping off the bus to a greeting from Kim, her Chesapeake Bay retriever, Samantha was greeted by a yardful of reporters holding cameras and notebooks. They were all taking her picture and asking her questions about the letter she had written and the answer she had just received.

Andropov's letter was more than two pages long. In his first paragraph, he compared Samantha to a fictional character named Becky Thatcher. In Mark Twain's novel, *Tom Sawyer*, Becky is a good friend of Tom's who takes part in several of the book's adventures. In one exciting scene, Tom and Becky get lost in a dark and dangerous cave, which is also the hiding place of a murderer.

Andropov wrote that Samantha seemed to him as "courageous and honest" as Becky. Samantha knew who Becky Thatcher was, and she was pleased by the comparison. "When you think of Yuri Andropov," Samantha told a reporter, "you really don't think about him having any humor." But Andropov's mention of Becky made Samantha think twice about what the Soviet leader might be like as a person. In fact, the whole thing sounded to her like "a letter from a friend."

How did Andropov respond to the difficult questions that Samantha had asked him in her letter? As an answer to her first question, he wrote: "Yes, Samantha, we in the Soviet Union are trying to do everything so that there will not be war between our countries, so that in general there will not be war on earth. This is what every Soviet man wants. This is what the great founder of our state Vladimir Lenin, taught us."

Then Andropov talked about how much the Soviet people had suffered during World War II. He reminded her that during that war, the United States and the Soviet Union had joined forces to defeat the Nazi armies. Then he answered Samantha's second question, the one asking why he wanted to conquer the world, or at least the United States. "No one in our country," wrote Andropov to Samantha, "neither workers, peasants, writers

Vladimir Lenin, pictured on this huge outdoor mural in the city of Leningrad, is a hero to the Soviet people.

nor doctors, neither grown-ups nor children, nor members of the government—wants either a big or 'little' war.''

''We want peace,'' he continued, ''—there is something that we are occupied with: growing wheat, building and inventing, writing books and flying into space. We want peace for ourselves and for all peoples of the planet. For our children and for you, Samantha.''

Perhaps the most exciting thing about the letter was an invitation to visit the Soviet Union that summer. ''You will find out about our country,'' Andropov wrote, ''visit an international children's camp—'Artek'—on the sea. And see for yourself: in the Soviet Union, everyone is for peace and friendship among peoples.''

All day, since she had read the letter in the morning, Samantha had been wondering whether she would actually go to the Soviet Union. But with all the reporters in the yard and flooding into the Smiths' bright kitchen, it was impossible to hold a family conference to decide! The phone was ringing constantly. Samantha was glad her parents and her best friend Lynn were around to help her handle all the commotion.

In the next few weeks Samantha and her family were, to say the least, kept busy. Luckily, Arthur Smith's classes at the University of Maine were over for the year. Samantha's father stayed home and answered the phone while his wife was at work and Samantha was at school. "I thought she might get some response from Andropov," he said, "but I never expected all this!" Arthur Smith also told reporters that Samantha had always been a good writer. "This," he said, "is just proof that letter-writing works and people do pay attention."

Articles about Samantha Smith and her letter to Yuri Andropov appeared in newspapers around the world. Here Samantha looks at an article about her in a Bulgarian newspaper. Many other articles are fastened to the wall behind her.

Samantha received many requests for interviews from all over the country. In New York, she appeared on the television programs "CBS Morning News," "Nightline," and the "Today" show. She and her mother also flew to California for Samantha's appearance on the "Tonight Show." Samantha's best friend Lynn went, too. "It was a super trip," said Samantha. "Johnny Carson was very nice even if he did kiss me. In California, everybody shakes your hand and then kisses you."

About a month had passed since Samantha received the letter from across the world. Although the Smiths still weren't sure they would travel to the Soviet Union, Samantha had become a familiar figure in the newspapers and on television. In May, after Samantha returned from California, the Smiths decided to accept Andropov's invitation. They would be visiting the Soviet Union in July.

Anatoly F. Dobrynin, the Soviet ambassador to the United States, sent them more details about the trip. It would be two weeks long, and would be paid for by the Soviet government. They would make three stops in the Soviet Union: Moscow, the Crimea—where Artek, the children's camp was located—and Leningrad. Samantha was happy that they would be visiting more than a children's camp. "I don't really like camps that much," she told a reporter.

Samantha finished fifth grade and practiced with her softball team. Except for the letters that kept pouring in from all over the world, her life returned to normal. Samantha had time to visit the library and learn more about the country she would be visiting in July.

In her letter to Andropov, Samantha referred to his country as "Russia." Russia, in fact, is the largest of the fifteen republics that make up the Union of Soviet Socialist Republics (U.S.S.R.), or the Soviet Union. Most Soviet people live in Russia, and the capital of the Soviet Union, Moscow, is in Russia. Although more than one hundred languages are spoken in the Soviet Union, Russian is the official language. For all these reasons, some people still refer to the Soviet Union as Russia, and call the people who live there Russians. But, as Samantha discovered through her library visits, it is more accurate to call them Soviets.

There is another reason for the confusion. Before 1922, Russia was the official name of the entire country. In 1917, the Russian king, or czar, was overthrown in a revolution. A group called the Bolsheviks, led by Vladimir Lenin, took over the government. Andropov mentioned Lenin in his letter to Samantha. In 1922, Lenin and the Bolshe-

These Soviet children represent the heritage of some of the fifteen republics in the world's largest country.

viks formed the Soviet Union and declared it a Communist country. They believed that the government should plan and run the nation's industries and farms and that the land should be owned by all the people. This is one of the ways that the Soviet Union differs from the United States.

Partly because their systems of government are so different, the United States and the Soviet Union have often regarded each other as enemies. In fact, during the 1950s, the two nations were said to be in a "Cold War." Although there wasn't any real fighting going on, there was a great deal of fear and mistrust on both sides. Both countries had nuclear weapons, and both were afraid that the other country would develop better weapons and start a war.

During the 1970s, steps were taken to slow down what had come to be known as the nuclear arms race. In 1972, President Nixon signed an agreement with Soviet President Brezhnev that limited the number of weapons each country could produce. In 1979, another agreement was reached, but since then progress has been slow. People in both the United States and the Soviet Union still fear a nuclear attack from the other country. It is this fear that Samantha Smith could not understand or accept.

Samantha and her father prepare to leave Maine on the first flight of their trip to the Soviet Union. Jane Smith, not in this picture, sits in a nearby seat on the small plane.

3 Peace for the rest of our lives

On June 29, Samantha celebrated her eleventh birthday. Less than two weeks remained until the trip! Samantha's grandmother Nonnie, and her cousin Tyler, arrived in Maine from North Carolina. They were going to stay at the Smiths' house and take care of Kim and the Smiths' cats.

Samantha was more and more excited, but she was also a bit nervous. From time to time she worried about whether the Soviet children she met would like her. Compared to meeting Soviet young people her own age, Samantha thought, writing to Andropov had been easy.

The adventure officially began on July 7, a sunny Thursday. Samantha got up early and dressed in comfortable clothes: light blue pants, a short-sleeved, striped green shirt, a favorite yellow sweater, and sneakers. Into the car went the family's suitcases and a picnic basket filled with gifts for the Smiths' Soviet hosts. These were T-shirts, buttons, tote bags, calendars, and stickers, all from Maine colleges and souvenir shops.

At the Augusta State Airport, Samantha and her parents said good-bye to their friends and to Nonnie and Tyler. They boarded a small plane for the first, and shortest, part of their long trip—from Augusta, Maine, to Boston, Massachusetts. From Boston the Smiths flew to Montreal, Canada. On that flight the pilot let Samantha try out the seat next to him in the cockpit. Next the plane flew nonstop for nine hours across the Atlantic Ocean and over Europe, arriving at Sheremetjevo Airport on Friday morning. In the lobby Samantha and her parents were greeted by two adult guides and a group of ten Soviet children. Samantha was welcomed with bouquets of flowers from her hosts.

On Saturday morning, the Smiths' Soviet hosts took them around Moscow in a whirlwind tour of the city's history and its famous buildings. Samantha discovered that, like Washington, D.C., Moscow contains the country's government buildings. Unlike Washington, though, most of these are grouped in a very old part of the city called the Kremlin. This section is entirely surrounded by a wall that was built in the fifteenth century—the same century that Columbus landed in America.

Inside the Kremlin, Samantha visited many of the palaces and gold-domed churches that date from the time when czars ruled the country. She also went into the apartment where Lenin lived in the last years of his life. The Soviets feel so strongly

about Lenin that his body is preserved in a tomb in Red Square, just outside the Kremlin Wall.

With the other visitors, Samantha filed by the glass case where Lenin's body lay. She found the tomb spooky and dark, and she was happier outside in the light on the square. Red Square is a large, open area where many of Moscow's parades and celebrations are held.

Wherever the Smiths went in Moscow, Samantha learned something more about the Soviet Union. What she learned on Saturday was interesting, but much of it—including a visit to the Tomb of the Unknown Soldier—was very serious. Aside from the brief meeting with children at the airport, Samantha hadn't had a chance to meet anyone her own age.

All that changed the next day when Samantha flew with her parents to the southern part of the

Starting their tour of Moscow, Samantha, Arthur, and Jane Smith explore the Kremlin.

Soviet Union known as the Crimea. This area is an outcropping of land surrounded almost entirely by the Black Sea. In the hills near Yalta, a town on the seacoast, lies the Artek Pioneer Camp that Andropov described to Samantha in his letter.

The Smiths' plane landed in the city of Simferopol, where a group of Young Pioneers from the camp met the American visitors. The Young Pioneers is a youth group for children aged nine to fourteen. It has many more members than either the U.S. Boy Scouts or Girl Scouts, and it is a part of the Communist party. The three-cornered red scarves that the campers wear around their necks stand for the connection between the Communist party and the Young Pioneers. The rest of their uniform consists of short-sleeved white shirts, navy blue caps, and navy blue shorts for the boys and skirts for the girls.

A Young Pioneer presents Samantha with a blue visitor's scarf to wear with the Pioneer uniform.

When Samantha arrived at Artek, the Soviet young people gave her a warm welcome. About a thousand children, all dressed in Pioneer uniforms, sat on bleachers in an outdoor theater by the sea. A thirteen-year-old girl named Natasha Kirishina read a statement welcoming Samantha to the camp. She also presented Samantha with a large round loaf of bread and a cup of salt, the traditional Russian symbols of welcome. Samantha didn't know how to respond to all the attention.

Samantha got over her shyness almost immediately. She was given a Pioneer uniform and a blue visitor's scarf, and over the next few days, she took part in almost all camp activities. Swimming was a big part of camp life. When a reporter asked her what her strongest impression of camp was, Samantha said it was "the sea, because in America, the lakes I swim in have lots of gunk on them."

Samantha enjoys a boat ride on the Black Sea with Natasha Kirishina, her best friend at Artek.

Samantha made a lot of friends at Artek. While her parents stayed in a hotel nearby, Samantha stayed in a dormitory with Natasha and nine other girls. The Soviet girls taught her songs and dances and asked her about life in the United States. "They were all interested in how I lived and sometimes at night we talked about peace, but it didn't really seem necessary because none of them hated America, and none of them ever wanted war," Samantha wrote. "It seemed strange even to talk about war when we all got along so well together."

Still, on the second afternoon she was there, Samantha and a group of her new friends went out in a boat to show their support for a peaceful world. Each of them threw a bottle containing a message into the Black Sea. Samantha's message read, "Hopefully, we will have peace for the rest of our lives."

On Wednesday, the Smiths left Artek for the northern city of Leningrad, and the campers left as well. It just so happened that Samantha's best friend at camp, Natasha, lived in Leningrad. Since she knew she would see Natasha again before she went home, Samantha felt a bit better about leaving the camp.

Samantha thought Natasha's city was beautiful. Located on the Gulf of Finland, Leningrad is the Soviet Union's second largest city, and its busiest port. Czar Peter the Great founded the city in 1703 and named it after himself: Saint Petersburg. In 1924, after the Russian Revolution, it was renamed for Vladimir Lenin. Still, many of Leningrad's buildings date from the time of Peter the Great. Two of the beautiful, enormous palaces that Samantha visited with Natasha were the Czar's summer and winter homes. His winter palace, built in what is now Leningrad's Revolution Square, has become the well-known Hermitage Museum.

Samantha also learned that much of Leningrad had been destroyed in World War II. At the burial

Samantha, her mother, and her friend Natasha stand by the fountains in front of Czar Peter the Great's Summer Palace.

place for almost half a million people who died during World War II, she saw an exhibit called "900 days of the Battle of Leningrad." For almost three years, the people of Leningrad were under attack by the German army. Many Soviet citizens died, but the Nazi forces never occupied the city.

A more cheerful part of Samantha's visit to Leningrad was her night at the Kirov Theater. Although she had taken ballet lessons for a year when she was small, Samantha had never before seen a professional dance performance. "I thought it would be boring, but it was terrific," she told a reporter afterward.

On Saturday, a week after they had left Moscow, Samantha and her parents took a midnight train from Leningrad. By the next morning, they arrived once more in the Soviet capital. Although they still did not know if Andropov would visit with them, Samantha had plenty to do. She toured the Bolshoi Ballet and the Moscow subways, rode a racing bicycle at the Krylatskoye Olympic Center, and attended performances at the Moscow Circus and the Moscow Puppet Theater. She visited with children at the Moscow Pioneer Palace and met Valentina Tereshkova, who in 1963 became the first woman in space.

On Wednesday, July 20, the day before the Smiths left for the United States, Samantha received a visit from Leonid Zamyatin, a Soviet government official. He told Samantha that Andropov was too busy meeting with the leader of Hungary to meet with her. Instead, she talked to Zamyatin about some of the issues that were in her letter. By that point in her trip, she felt far less worried about the chances of war between the two countries. At a news conference in Moscow the next morning,

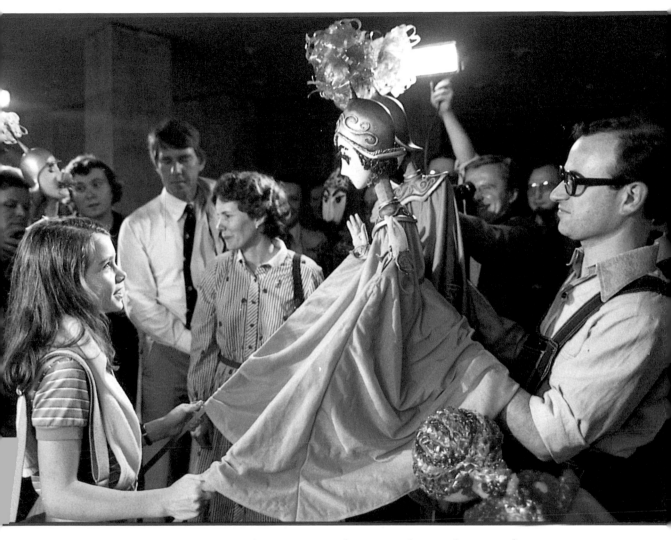

At Moscow's Puppet Theater, Samantha gets a close-up lesson on how to move the parts of a puppet.

Shortly after returning home to Maine, Samantha Smith receives the key to the city of Manchester.

Samantha said, "People who have been to the Soviet Union know that the Soviet people don't want war at all, they just want peace."

Back in Manchester, Maine, Samantha's grandmother baked cookies for a homecoming party. Her cousin Tyler draped the Smiths' house with red, white, and blue streamers and hung a "Welcome Home" banner on the roof. The rest of the town prepared for the annual Old Manchester Day Parade, which was scheduled for that Saturday.

On Friday, the parade's guest of honor flew into Augusta State Airport. More than three hundred people were there to greet her, cheering and waving balloons and banners. By this time, Samantha was a bit tired of all the attention she had received in the past couple of weeks. "I'm happy to be getting home to regular things," she said. "It's nice to visit, but I'd rather live in my hometown."

During a trip to Japan, Samantha visits the printing section of the Yomiuri

4 People can get along

Although Samantha's trip to the Soviet Union ended on July 22, 1983, it led to many new experiences over the next two years. On the one hand, Samantha finished sixth grade at Manchester Elementary School, and seventh grade at Maranacook Community School in Readfield. She listened to rock music—her favorite musicians were Prince and Huey Lewis and the News—and played in Manchester's softball league. But she was also appearing frequently on television, writing *Journey to the Soviet Union* with her father's help, and giving speeches in places as far away as Nevada and Japan.

Five months after returning from the Soviet Union, Samantha and her mother took another trip halfway around the world, this time to Japan. On their ten-day trip, they visited the cities of Tokyo and Kyoto. They joined children from all over the world at the Children's International Symposium for the Twenty-first Century in Kobe.

At this meeting were four members of the U.S. children's news organization called The Children's Express. Steven Naplan, a thirteen-year-old reporter from Massachusetts, talked about the speeches he had heard in Kobe. Almost everyone who spoke, no matter where they came from, shared Samantha's worry about the threat of nuclear war. Even though the meeting was supposed to be about science, Steven said the speakers "seemed to be a lot more concerned about how far we'll get in life than how far we'll get in space."

In her speech at Kobe, Samantha proposed that Soviet and U.S. leaders exchange granddaughters for two weeks every year. A president, she figured, "wouldn't want to send a bomb to a country his granddaughter was visiting." She also thought such a plan would help create international understanding so that by the year 2001 "everyone could be friends."

At home in Manchester, Samantha reached out to students who seemed jealous of her success. One friend who shared Samantha's locker at school said, "She didn't act like she was different from us, she acted the same as everyone else did." Her school advisor, William Preble, thought that she handled her success well. "She was such a normal kid in light of all that fame and fortune," he said. At a peace meeting in her home state, Samantha said that her trip to the Soviet Union had taught her an important lesson: if they try hard enough, people can get along. "I don't know why grown-

ups can't get along," she told the applauding
audience.

In January 1984, Samantha received an offer to
host a television show for the Disney Channel, a
cable television network. Broadcast in February,
the program was called "Samantha Smith Goes to
Washington." On the show, Samantha interviewed
Democratic candidates for the 1984 presidential
election, including George McGovern and the Rev-
erend Jesse Jackson. It was a chance for her to ask
the candidates about her own concerns.

To find out what was on the minds of other
American young people, Samantha visited class-
rooms in Boston and Washington. She also took
many of the questions she asked the candidates
from the thousands of letters she had received
since her trip. So, in a way, she was acting as a
representative of children from around the world.

"I never thought it would result in all this," Samantha said in an interview that summer. A year and many more TV appearances later, Samantha received yet another invitation—this time from Linda Bloodworth, the writer of a new ABC adventure series called "Lime Street." Linda said she had seen Samantha on the "Today" show, and asked her to fly to California to try out for a part on "Lime Street." Samantha jumped at the chance, even though her frequent trips away from Manchester meant she "kept missing out on stuff" at home. Already she had missed the school's Christmas dance and her best friend's birthday party.

Happily, though, Samantha got the part of Elizabeth Culver on the show. "I thought I did really terrible," she said about her tryout. "I was almost in tears. When Linda came over, though, she told me that I had the [part in the] series."

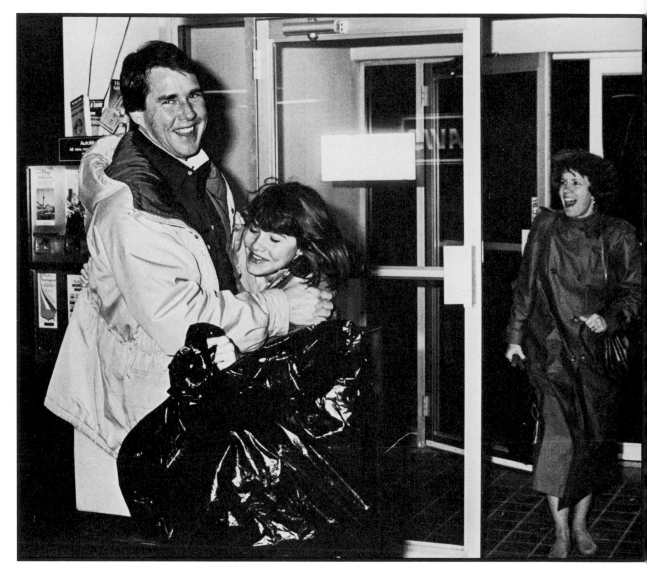

Returning home from California after acting for "Lime Street," Samantha gets a big hug from her father.

Waiting to board a plane at the airport in Maine, Samantha studies her lines for an episode of "Lime Street."

Samantha was offered the part in May 1985. The filming of the first four episodes took place that summer, after she had finished the seventh grade. The show's main character, J.G. Culver, was played by Robert Wagner. Culver was an insurance investigator who traveled throughout the world solving mysteries. His home, though, was a horse farm in Virginia, where his two daughters—played by Samantha and eight-year-old Maia Brewton—lived with their grandfather.

The first four "Lime Street" episodes were filmed mostly in Virginia. Samantha put in long hours of work on the set there, but said she was having "great fun" learning about acting. In fact, after the episodes in Virginia were filmed, she decided she wanted to become an actress. She especially liked getting to know Robert Wagner. "It's easier to work with someone who knows what he's doing," she told a reporter on a visit home. "He was like my own father. He helped me and Maia out a lot, giving out tips on acting. He's a sweet man—great with kids."

By this time, Samantha's real-life father had stopped teaching to help manage his daughter's career. He jokingly referred to himself as Samantha's "baggage carrier," and went with her on most of her speaking and acting journeys. When it was announced that the fifth episode of "Lime Street" would be set in London, England, he decided to go along while Samantha's mother stayed in Manchester. The trip there was uneventful, and the episode successfully filmed. Afterward Samantha and her father headed for home.

They arrived in Boston on the evening of August 25, 1985, and boarded a Bar Harbor Airlines flight to Augusta, where Jane Smith was waiting to

pick them up. The weather was cloudy, but not cloudy enough to signal trouble. But for some reason, still unclear, the flight did not follow its scheduled path and headed toward the Auburn-Lewiston Municipal Airport. Half a mile from the airport, the plane crashed and exploded. Samantha, her father, and everyone else on board were killed.

Samantha and her father share a moment together before leaving on one of their trips.

САМАНТА СМИТ

1985

5 К ПОЧТА СССР

The Soviet government issued this stamp to honor Samantha Smith's work to
achieve greater understanding among the people and nations of the world.

5 We will find the way

Since Samantha's death in 1985, people all over the world have paid tribute to her and what she accomplished. A family friend said that Samantha would be remembered for "the clearness of her thinking, the willingness to question, the eager friendliness and the lovingness she showed . . . to other people." The Soviet government has issued a stamp with her picture, and has named a diamond, a flower, a planet, and a mountain for her. A Soviet woman named her baby after Samantha. In Minnesota, a television station broadcast a children's television program in memory of Samantha. The program was shown at the same time in the Soviet Union.

The greatest tribute, though, came from the people of Maine. After more than a year of planning and fund-raising, a life-size bronze statue of Samantha Smith took its place near the Maine state capitol in Augusta. The statue shows Samantha releasing a dove, an international symbol, or sign, of peace. A bear cub at Samantha's side is a symbol of both the Maine black bear and the Soviet Union. A plaque on the front of the statue bears these words: "Samantha Reed Smith, June 29, 1972—August 25, 1985, Maine's young ambassador of goodwill."

Money to build "The People of Maine's Memorial to Samantha Smith" came from schoolchildren and companies in Maine and all over the country. "The idea for the memorial came as a response to the people of the community who expressed a strong need to do something to honor

Jane Smith stands beside "The People of Maine's Memorial to Samantha Smith" near the Maine state capitol in Augusta.

Samantha Smith and her work for peace," said project coordinator Glenn Michaels. "The model of the statue was displayed in seven Maine cities, allowing thousands of people to participate in the fund-raising," explained Michaels. Project artist Glenn Hines, a long-time friend of the Smith family, worked with Jane Smith on the design.

During the brief official ceremony at the state capitol, Maine Governor Joseph E. Brennan and Jane Smith spoke about the statue and its meaning. Members of the Soviet American Memorial Exchange (Project S.A.M.E.) from Maranacook Community School also took part in the ceremony. Project S.A.M.E. is a group of students who were classmates and friends of Samantha Smith. Their purpose is to carry on the spirit of goodwill and international understanding that was started by Samantha.

For Jane Smith, the grief of losing her husband and her daughter in a single accident was difficult to bear. "When I think of what will never be," she said, "I get weepy, but I'm trying to look at the future in a positive way." She decided that she wanted to get involved in something that really mattered to her—something that is best expressed by Samantha's own words: "Sometimes I still worry that the next day will be the last day of the Earth. But with more people thinking about the problems of the world, I hope that someday soon we will find the way to world peace. Maybe someone will show us the way."

In October 1985, Jane Smith established the Samantha Smith Foundation to encourage friendship among the world's young people and to educate people everywhere about peace. The foundation has sponsored an exchange between the

Joan Benoit Samuelson, the Olympic marathon champion from Maine, appears with Jane Smith to announce "Joanie's Jam for Sam." All the money from the sale of this handmade Maine blueberry jam goes to support the work of the Samantha Smith Foundation.

In 1986 Jane Smith returned to the Soviet Union with a group of Samantha's classmates. Here she is greeted by Natasha Kirishina (left) in Leningrad's "House of Friendship and Peace with the Peoples of Foreign Countries."

United States and the Soviet Union. In the summer of 1986, a group of Samantha's classmates from Project S.A.M.E., accompanied by Jane Smith, retraced the steps that Samantha took on her trip. In August 1987, a group of Soviet teenagers made a return visit to the United States, including a summer camp in Maine. The foundation has also held conferences to show how to start peace education programs. In the future, many more activities are planned to help create understanding between individuals, and so between countries.

"Each generation," Jane Smith has said, "contributes a building block for the next generation. As individuals, we are the particles of earth from which the blocks are formed. I hope Samantha and Arthur have helped us realize how important each one of us can be."

INDEX

ABOUT THE AUTHOR

Anne Galicich, a free-lance writer, travels frequently to Maine and has a strong interest in Samantha Smith's native state. Ms. Galicich first heard of Samantha while teaching English to junior and senior high school students at Horace Mann School in New York City. "In this nuclear age," says the author, "Samantha Smith, who took such clear and simple steps toward understanding, is an inspiration to children and adults alike."

Ms. Galicich is a graduate of Stanford University and attended the Bread Loaf School of English, Middlebury College, and the Dodge Faculty Development Seminar in Women's Studies, Wellesley College. She resides in New York City.